Being the Change

Profiles from
Our Servant Leadership Learning
Community

Ann McGee-Cooper
Gary Looper
Duane Trammell

Foreword by Jack Lowe

Afterword by Don M. Frick

ANN MCGEE-COOPER AND ASSOCIATES, INC.
DALLAS

BEING THE CHANGE: PROFILES FROM OUR
SERVANT LEADERSHIP LEARNING COMMUNITY
An AMCA Book/ May 2007

ISBN 978-0-9795149-0-6

Quantity Sales
Available at special quantity discounts when purchased by bulk. Call Ann
McGee-Cooper and Associates, Inc. at 214-357-8550 or e-mail Carol Haddock
at carol@amca.com

Dedication

To past and present members of the Servant Leadership Learning Community who have joined together to envision, explore, and engage in leaderful practices. For seven years, you have inspired us to continue learning how to "be the change" we want to see in the world.

Organizational Members:

Ann McGee-Cooper and Associates, Inc.

Balfour Beatty
      (formerly Centex Construction Company)

Bill Priest Institute for Economic Development

Carrollton Police Department

Celebration Restaurant & Catering

Grocery Supply Company Enterprises, Inc.

lauckgroup

Parkland Health & Hospital System

PCI the data company

Southwest Airlines

TDIndustries

Tempo Mechanical Services

TXU Communications

US Cellular

Contents

Foreword

By Jack Lowe

Board Chair, TDIndustries
Board Chair, Robert K. Greenleaf Center for Servant Leadership
Board of Trustees
President, Dallas Independent School District Board of Trustees

My dad, who founded TDIndustries after serving in the Army Air Corps during World War II, was a natural servant-leader and was my role model and hero. About 1970, when he discovered Bob Greenleaf's pamphlet, *The Servant as Leader,* it gave clarity to his thinking on leadership. He became much more interested in the culture of TD than in its financial outcomes. After much dialogue among the Partners at TD, servant leadership was embraced as our model for leadership and for creating the foundation of trust on which we have operated. Dad was also very active in the community, especially with issues involving race relations. He took Bob's pamphlet into every situation and organization, and today Dallas has more organizations practicing servant leadership than any other large metropolitan area in the United States.

In the mid 1970s, my parents met Ann McGee-Cooper. Dad introduced her to servant leadership and invited her to create learning experiences at TD that would help us grow everyone's leadership capacity. Over the last 30-plus years, Ann and her associates have influenced the lives of thousands of TD Partners and helped us create a leaderful organization and a great place to work. We always expected business results from our Partners. We learned from our friends at Synovus Financial Corporation in Columbus, Georgia, to place an equal expectation on servant leadership. Today our expectations of every TD Partner include business results *and* servant leadership. We will go to great lengths to help Partners strengthen their capability in each area, but over time if you can't deliver good results in both, you shouldn't work for TD.

> After 30 years, TD still hasn't produced one perfect
> servant-leader, but AMCA has helped a lot of us become
> much better leaders.

Ann McGee-Cooper and Associates has impacted many organizations in Dallas over the last 30 years, and some of their stories await you in this book. The real power of AMCA's work has been in knitting together these organizations into a learning community. We all have shared successes and setbacks and learned together under the gentle mentoring, coaching, and teaching of AMCA.

Ann has also been a great supporter of the Greenleaf Center for Servant Leadership. She has served on its board in its formative years, presented at most of its annual conferences, and led the planning of the program for the conference in Dallas in June 2007.

Finally, a personal word about Ann. She has been a confidant, coach, and encourager through some challenging times at TD, as well as in my personal life. Ann's presence in my life is a great blessing.

Introduction

"Create Dangerously": The Alchemy of Love

It's the first Servant Leadership Learning Community (SLLC) session of 2007, and a roomful of 30 leaders sit in stunned silence as a police sergeant begins his story.

"Five years ago I was a major troublemaker in our department. I hated everything about my job and every minute of it. I came to work every day with a deep resolve to do all I could to make everyone around me just as miserable as I was, and I got good at it. So good at stirring the pot that soon it began to impact my home life.

"Then, I got lucky. A patrol sergeant invited me in for a heart-to-heart talk. He confronted me with who I had become, but more important, he told me that he believed I could change. He helped me see that the talents I was using to create distrust, suspicion, and rancor among my colleagues could be put to better use. He knew I had become a major disruption, yet he encouraged me to change. He helped me see how I was trapping myself in a misery that was destroying my life.

"Once I began to change, Chief Tristan became a major supporter who never looked back or held a grudge. He not only forgave me for my past, he worked to support the new direction I was working hard to learn. With his support and my willingness to work hard at changing for the better, I was eventually promoted to sergeant! I have a great debt to this man, and he will always have my loyalty."

Tears welled up in most of us as we felt the profound and fragile gift this man offered back to each of us as leaders.

This is not a therapy or self-help group. It's a "help others" group that evolved from some remarkable companies in the Dallas area. All around us, people long to make a positive difference with their lives. Would we dare to reach out with love and "create dangerously" as servant-leaders? This is the challenge we come to explore together each quarter in our SLLC.

Albert Camus, an artist and a man Robert Greenleaf considered a prophet, challenged each person to confront the life [one] has been given as an opportunity for greatness, "like Sisyphus, to accept [one's] rock and find [one's] happiness in dealing with it." The last university lecture given by Camus was titled, "Create Dangerously."

Robert Greenleaf tells how he derived the term, "servant leadership." "As I ponder the fusing of servant and leader it seems a dangerous creation: dangerous for the natural servant to become a leader, dangerous for the leader to be servant first, and dangerous for a follower to insist that he be led by a servant."

We find this same life experience again and again in the SLLC as we dare to journey deeper into what it means to be servant-leaders committed to grow communities that learn.

We at AMCA, Inc. have been part of the servant leadership movement for the past 30 years through hands-on research, interviews of leaders, direct observation of workers, and living what we teach. We have spoken on this subject at numerous conferences, and many people have asked for a resource that shows what servant leadership looks like in the workplace. While much has been written on the philosophy, we are far too short of examples of principles in practice.

We have been amazed by the servant leadership work accomplished in our SLLC organizations. In the following chapters we offer their inspiring stories. At the end of each chapter, we provide questions or insights to ponder on your own personal or organizational servant leadership journey. And, a final chapter tells the story of how and why we co-created the SLLC.

It is our hope that these snapshots of servant leadership in action will help answer the lingering question many of you have asked, "What does servant leadership look like in day-to-day organizational life?"

CHAPTER

Going the Distance:
A 30-Year Partnership of the Spirit with TDIndustries

TDIndustries is a lifecycle provider of facility services and specialty construction. With offices in Dallas, Fort Worth, Houston, Austin, San Antonio, Denver, and Phoenix, TD employs more than 1350 Partners with $234 million in revenue in 2006. Founded in 1946, TD has adopted and practiced servant leadership for more than 30 years. TD's "leaderful" culture has given it a unique place in the construction industry and propelled it into Fortune *magazine's "100 Best Companies to Work for in America" Hall of Fame. TD's mission:*

> *We are committed to*
> *providing outstanding career opportunities*
> *by exceeding our Customers' expectations*
> *through continuous aggressive improvement.*

This is a story about serendipity, synergy, and synchronicity. Thirty years ago, three lives converged in a chance meeting. Their collective calling gave birth to a vision that has transformed three generations of leaders.

Robert K. Greenleaf rose to a challenge from his college economics professor to find ways to transform dysfunctional businesses and

11

organizations by finding ways to address their ego-led hierarchies. Four decades later, he captured the imagination of many with his seminal essay, *The Servant as Leader*. In it, he thoughtfully delineated a practical philosophy of leadership that was dramatically different from the traditional model of the "egocentric" or "boss" paradigm.

Jack Lowe, Sr., a natural servant leader and founder of an air-conditioning equipment distributor, construction, and services company in Dallas, had a vision that a company could be more than a job and a paycheck. He was committed to engaging his *Employees as *Partners, practicing servant leadership to bring mutual trust and a servant's heart into business. He envisioned a leaderful organization in which every person awakened their full potential and responsibilities both as leaders and servants of others.

NOTE: The authors have adopted Southwest Airlines' practice of capitalizing "Employee" and "Customers" and TDIndustries' style of capitalizing "Partner" to reflect their respectful terminology.

I (Ann) was a very lucky young teacher with the belief that every life has a gift of unique genius and every person has the potential to learn and transform. Jack Lowe, Sr. invited me to help create a servant-led company and the result has been a 30-year partnership of the spirit. My life continues to be transformed by these two incredibly inspiring servant-leaders, Jack Lowe, Sr. and Robert K. Greenleaf.

The Legacy of a Natural Servant-Leader

Jack Lowe, Sr., founder and president of Texas Distributors (now TDIndustries), changed the face of Dallas by the remarkable level of trust in his relationships. Because of his extraordinary servant leadership, alliances formerly thought impossible were created, benefiting the entire city. An outstanding example was Jack's capacity to bring racial groups filled with distrust into a shared plan to integrate the Dallas public schools. In his honor, a new public school in the Dallas Independent School District has been named after this man who forged a lasting trust.

Jack Lowe, Sr.

In 1970, Greenleaf wrote *The Servant as Leader*. Jack came across a copy of the book not long afterwards and liked it so much that he began buying copies by the box and passing them out to Employees, the Biracial Council and various other civic organizations as well as business friends at his church. Greenleaf became curious about who was buying his book in bulk and why. A phone call began a long and deep friendship in which each man drew on his intuitive belief that more respectful, effective ways to grow leadership existed.

For two years, Jack Lowe and Linda Wyatt Smithey, his executive assistant, met with small groups of Employees in his home to discuss Greenleaf's essay and how they might apply it in their work together. In a memoir, Smithey wrote, "Harriet Lowe was a great contributor in those meetings. Here we were in the home of the president, and his wife was making lunch for us. In a lot of ways, he was saying, 'I really want you here. I want you to be a part of the family, not just the company.'"

Together, they created the People Objective from Linda's notes from dialogues with every Employee.

"Each and every TD person to feel successful as a person – as a total person – with one's co-workers, family, friends, community, God, and self. Among other things, this means one must feel growth, must feel individually important … and it requires of oneself a high order of responsibility and self-discipline."

"If through oversight or neglect or just not caring much, we fail to do what we can to help even one person in this objective, it's really a bad failure. For this concept to be real, it must be total. There must be no one excluded."

After presenting this to the Employees, they also came up with some "Yardsticks."

1. Be honest.
2. Think and act like a manager.
3. Help create profits.
4. Help create satisfied Customers.
5. Be understanding and helpful. Put yourself in the other person's shoes.

Several years later, some of the Employees felt that the company was not following through on the People Objective and Yardsticks. That's when Jack's storied breakfast sessions began. Again, with small groups, he met to openly talk about the heart and soul of Texas

Distributors. Out of these sessions came an organic list of characteristics that continue to guide the company.

TD Leadership Values

These values were inspired by Robert Greenleaf's book *The Servant as Leader,* in which he expressed how people can and should work together to grow a company. If the organization is to live up to its basic values and mission, a key ingredient will be the leadership provided by a very large number of us. Simply and plainly defined

- leaders are people who have followers. They have earned recognition and respect.

- leaders are first servants of those they lead. They are teachers, sources of information and knowledge, and standard setters, more than givers of directions and disciplinarians.

- leaders see things through the eyes of their followers. They put themselves in others' shoes and help them make their dreams come true.

- leaders do not say, "Get going." Instead, they say, "Let's go!" and lead the way. They do not walk behind with a whip; they are out in front with a banner.

- leaders assume that their followers are working with them. They consider others Partners in the work and see to it that they share in the rewards. They glorify the team spirit!

- leaders are people builders. They help those around them to grow because a leader realizes that stronger people make stronger organizations.

- leaders do not hold people down, they lift them up. They reach out their hands to help their followers scale the peaks.

- leaders have faith in people. They believe in them. They have found that others rise to their expectations.

- leaders use their heart as well as their head. After they have looked at the facts with their head, they let their heart take a look too.

- leaders keep their eyes on high goals. They are self-starters. They create plans and set them in motion. They are persons of thought and action – both dreamers and doers.

- leaders are faced with many hard decisions, including balancing fairness to an individual with fairness to the group. This sometimes requires a "weeding out" of those in the group who, over a period of time, do not measure up to the group needs of dependability, productivity, and safety.

- leaders have a sense of humor. They are not stuffed shirts. They can laugh at themselves. They have a humble spirit.

- leaders can be led. They are not interested in having their own way, but in finding the best way. They have an open mind.

Six months before he died, Jack suggested three other ideas that might be added to the company's list of purposes: To serve God. To serve our fellow [beings]. To build a group of people who work together in friendship and love.

Ashley Cheshire in *A Partnership of the Spirit*

These words capture the spirit and conviction of an exemplary servant-leader who gave his life for the benefit of Partners at TD and the City of Dallas.

In 1976, I (Ann) was invited to be the keynote speaker at a national conference for religious educators, chaired by Harriet Lowe, Jack's wife. Jack attended the conference and invited me to talk with him about the dream he held for his company. He asked me to read a copy of *The Servant as Leader,* by Robert K. Greenleaf, then to come back and share my thoughts. When I returned, fascinated and inspired by what I had read, I explained how the tenets of servant leadership were parallel to what I believed about effective teaching: the most effective teachers lived what they taught, believed deeply in the unlimited capacity of every student, and used experiential learning to make learning fun and engaging. Making it safe to ask questions, explore differences of opinion, and engage in honest dialogue was essential to achieving lasting changes in behavior. In addition, interactive experiences became the basis for discovering more effective ways to team and lead.

As a professor at Southern Methodist University, I founded and directed a research project that became a lab school pioneering highly innovative learning techniques. The Experimental Arts Program was also known for work with students of all ages using accelerated learning. This highly validated technique brought learning to a deeper level, more quickly, with a higher level of retention. I taught graduate students (all experienced teachers) to use these techniques successfully in situations where students frequently experienced failure and, as a result, had low self-esteem. By making learning fun, engaging all the senses, and creating a safe atmosphere where success became the norm, abstract concepts could be understood and applied with extraordinary results.

Jack knew that the concepts of servant leadership were abstract and went against traditional management theory and beliefs. And he realized that craft workers didn't do well in traditional academic settings. But he thought my nontraditional teaching techniques and strong belief that everyone could excel might fit his vision to bring servant leadership into the lives, hearts, and daily work habits of every manager and Partner at TD.

In the beginning I collaborated with Steve Saunders, a bright young intern who was at that time Jack's executive assistant. Steve took me to several construction job sites for a first-hand look at the work environments challenging leaders at TD. Then, together, we began to integrate Steve's knowledge of the business, Greenleaf's concepts of servant leadership, and my experience creating a learning environment where everyone could succeed.

Robert K. Greenleaf: Mentor and Friend

Not long after beginning this partnership with TD, I was invited to Philadelphia to visit Bob and Esther Greenleaf at Crosslands Quaker Retirement Community. I brought pages of questions that became the basis for long conversations with Bob (many of which were taped). Over the next 10 years, there were several visits, phone calls, and letters. I was lucky enough to have Bob as a patient coach, mentor, and friend, guiding my efforts to fully understand servant leadership and bring it into the work with Partners at TD.

Robert Greenleaf and Ann McGee-Cooper

16

Bob was an incredible listener who took my thinking to a deeper level. He built on what I knew and helped me discover the power of silence, reflection, and not knowing. I only wish I could have a second go at being his student. He was so far out in front that only now, three decades later, am I catching up to what he was trying to help me discover.

Bob had a keen sense of humor, an intense curiosity, and a gift for asking the kinds of questions that opened new doors of wondering. He frequently baffled and delighted me. Just when I thought I understood where he was leading me, he would surprise me with a totally different idea.

For example, one day we were talking about trust. I had learned from my father to prudently withhold trust until the other person had proven trustworthy. Greenleaf suggested that I might want to rethink this assumption. When a person you trust and admire has faith in you beyond where you currently are, they give you a new vision to grow into and own. The capacity to create an expectation of excellence and then trust another to live up to it was a new idea to me. And yet, as I reflected on my life, I realized that in more than one instance I had made a significant leap in performance because someone I admired believed in me, and I did not want to let that person down. Learning to trust first opens the possibility for enhanced performance and breaks the negative chain of self-fulfilling prophecy.

On another visit I was talking nonstop, eager to learn as much as I possibly could in the short time we had together. Bob often found other, more creative ways to reveal new insights, as he did on this day. As I talked, he quietly reached out, took my hand, and led me outside in the sunshine to a wooden bench where we sat in a long silence. It was clear that more talking wasn't appropriate.

Then he began to explain that his Quaker background had given him two valuable gifts. The first was, "Don't speak unless you can improve upon the silence." I was stunned. What could this mean? For me silence was an opportunity to fill something empty, my time to talk. I had never considered that it might have value in and of itself. And just when I was grasping the idea that long periods of silence might lead to a deeper level of insight, Bob explained the second gift. "When Spirit moves within you, you must give

> it your voice. These two create a tension within which true
> dialogue emerges."

We sat for a long while as these thoughts took root. Bob was a
thoughtful person who had a gift for saying much with few words.
While I may never fit this description, this conversation helped me
begin to discover new possibilities.

Bob was a practical businessman as well as a futurist. Consider his
15 criteria for running a sound, long-run business.

15 Criteria of a Sound Long-Run Business

1. Make a satisfactory profit.
2. Protect our assets and use them efficiently – provide capital and
   access to capital for the future.
3. Maintain good stockholder relations.
4. Maintain and improve our position in the industry and the
   economy.
5. Develop new products, new fields, new techniques, and new
   demands.
6. Conform fully with laws and ethical standards.
7. Satisfy our Customers and keep them sound.
8. Maintain good relations with competitors to improve the
   industry.
9. Earn the respect of communities in which we operate.
10. Favorably influence the climate in which all business operates.
11. Effect growth of people in the business – in terms of morale,
    attitude, ability, initiative, self-reliance.
12. Effect welfare of people in the business – in terms of economic
    security, health, safety, family, stability, community
    responsibility.
13. Improve our knowledge of and control over our business.
14. Contribute something to the art of management.
15. Provide for future top management of the business.

Robert K. Greenleaf *in On Becoming a Servant-Leader*

A Company for Bold Dreams

In 1982, Duane Trammell joined me to form a new company, Ann
McGee-Cooper and Associates, Inc. (AMCA). Together, we chose to
base it on the culture of servant leadership we found so inspiring at TD.
Our vision was to become servant-leaders who inspired our clients to
claim bold dreams through "whole-brained" balance. Learning to teach

through the whole brain was the secret of accelerated learning and a process we integrated into everything we designed for TD.

A Unique Partnership

Most consulting relationships don't last for 30 years, much less grow into a deeply committed partnership that goes beyond a formal contractual agreement. Over the years, TD has found numerous ways to grow and strengthen the small consulting team of futurists that is Ann McGee-Cooper and Associates. And, AMCA is committed to go the second and third mile routinely to insure success for TD. Here are some of the unique dimensions that define this highly synergistic partnership:

1. **From the very beginning, TD invested in growing AMCA as Partners.** It is unusual for a company to reach beyond its Employees and provide training and development opportunities for vendors. Yet, AMCA has always been invited to attend all the leadership development and training offered to TD Partners. This included opportunities to work directly with Stephen Covey, Bill Guillory, and Tom Peters. There were also classes on quality, continuous performance improvement, Spanish, and others. By growing us, AMCA could not only add more value, but also integrate the curriculums we were designing with the other skills being taught and practiced.

2. **TD's CEO (or another senior leader) has always personally come to kick off and close the servant leadership classes.** It's remarkable that a top company leader consistently invested the time to welcome and challenge each class going through servant leadership development. The shared goal was to make sure that Employees knew the learning they experienced came directly from the cultural aspirations of their

Jack Lowe, Jr.

leaders and Partners. It was not something from outside or "off the shelf." Toward the end of the day the senior leader rejoined the class to listen in, provide a vision going forward, and challenge each Partner to live as a servant-leader. Only then could a culture of trust, respect, and a great place to work become a reality.

In 1980, when Jack Lowe earned the CEO role at TD, he continued to espouse his father's philosophy of servant leadership. Jack relates his personal perspective on the role of servant leadership at TD:

"Bob Greenleaf, in *The Servant as Leader,* describes a new kind of leadership which puts serving others, including Partners, Customers, and Community, as the highest priority. This servant leadership built the trusting relationship which got us through difficult times together and provided the foundation for using the tools of quality to aggressively improve the ways we serve our Customers. Servant leadership builds the trust which allows us to work together successfully as we face a continually changing future."

Earning and maintaining the highest levels of trust was the foundation upon which both Jack and his father did business. One of Jack's special gifts was to build TD as a business. Yet he did so from a primary commitment to servant leadership. Even in financial downturns, Jack never wavered in his commitment to grow the people as well as the business. He comments today, "The return on investment (ROI) on really good leadership development is almost infinite. Partners who spend a day away from their job in personal development feel so valued that they do ten days' work in the next nine days. After that all the gains from the experience are free."

In January 2006, after several years of careful succession planning, Harold MacDowell became the third CEO at TD. Promoted from within, Harold now begins classes by sharing his own servant leadership stories from the past 20 years as the foundation for his new role. His message is compelling: "I'm convinced that our collective commitment to servant leadership enhances the shared trust

Harold MacDowell

that produces strong business results. It is my expectation that each of you will join me in this commitment." Harold also tells funny, humbling stories of sobering mistakes that have helped him mature as a compassionate leader. Humor and humility are cornerstones of TD's culture, and in his new role, Harold works hard to connect openly with everyone. Each leader is unique, yet what sets TD apart is the seamless commitment to making trust the foundation on which a great business and a great workplace are built.

3. **AMCA worked closely with top leaders from TD to recruit sponsors for every class.** The evaluations/feedback gathered after every class clearly indicated a greater need to link servant leadership principles back to the workplace. We needed a TD leader in the class who would help reinforce the concepts by providing specific examples of how and why servant leadership was a better, more productive way to do business.

4. **TD leaders were committed to responding to concerns about leadership behavior brought forward during servant leadership classes.** The senior sponsor and/or the People Department followed up on class questions. Sometimes, a participant asked, "Has my supervisor ever attended this class?" When class sponsors heard this, they knew we all had a lot of work to do getting every manager and supervisor to understand the importance of "walking the talk." Soon, an advanced servant leadership class was added so all managers could renew and continue growing their skills.

5. **AMCA co-developed the servant leadership curriculum with TD.** From the beginning, the servant leadership curriculum evolved from a thorough assessment of recommendations from all levels of leaders. Periodically, the team at AMCA met with representatives from TD to learn what they thought was most important, as well as their desired outcomes. From these meetings, we collected current success stories to illustrate the learning skills. We then added quotations from current leaders explaining why servant leadership is not only a more successful way of doing business, but also the best path toward creating a great place to work.

As a result of our research, we established four goals for a curriculum:

1. Share Greenleaf's concepts about serving people.
2. Provide practical "how-to's" of good supervision.

3. Educate about TD's past and continuing investment in servant leadership.

4. Intersperse activities and conversations that allow TD Partners time to dialogue and reflect on how they are doing on these important management/supervision activities.

Careful thought is given to the recognition of TD's legacy of servant leadership practice. Each workbook is filled with pictures of TD Partners doing their jobs. Section openers contain not only quotes from Greenleaf, but quotes from TD leaders sharing their philosophy of servant leadership. To accomplish our last goal of allowing time for Partners to share how they are doing with servant leadership, we use short videos, table discussions, reflective imaging and team activities, role play, simulations, and Customer problem-solving situations created by TD Partners. Rich dialogue and deep insights come from these interactive experiences.

Without question, the positive momentum of this process comes from the participants. Even though we are charged with designing and leading this process, we always come as students, create our own personal action plan and are accountable for our growth. The continuing transformation of all parties creates a synergy which grows stronger each year.

6. **TD participants proposed a "90-day review."** One of our sponsors asked the class, "How can we make sure that we don't forget to practice these great new skills as we all rush back into our work?" One Partner suggested that the class reconvene for 90 minutes in 90 days with a promise to be accountable for one new skill or improvement from their personal action plan. The goal was 100 percent attendance and 100 percent reporting on at least one new area of improvement. This was so successful that it has become a norm for all the leadership classes at TD.

7. **In 1998, based on a growing number of new Partners who spoke English as a second language, AMCA and TD together invested in getting the curriculum materials translated into Spanish.**

8. **We practiced win/win/win teaming.** When either AMCA or TD was in trouble, the other went the extra mile. For example, Jack Lowe, Jr. provided a number of business references to help AMCA find Dallas clients and build a strong, local presence. And when TD was in tight financial situations, AMCA found

ways to keep the classes going on a very slim budget. We have worked hard to limit the class size to 35 so that every Partner gets special attention and time for their questions to be explored. TD has always made growing its people a top priority, even when times are tough.

9. **As outside interest in servant leadership grew, AMCA and TD made the classes a lab school for servant leadership and allowed for a limited number of guests to observe or participate in the classes.** These guests included not only subcontractors working closely with TD, but also school board members, principals, and top leaders of other community nonprofit groups such as the YMCA and Red Cross. Together we teamed with the Greenleaf Center to make our curriculum available worldwide to those interested in servant leadership.

10. **Based on its long-term partnership with TD, AMCA created 14 learning modules to teach servant leadership so that anyone, anywhere, had access to high quality materials at a very reasonable price.**

11. **Early in the process, we worked to integrate servant leadership principles into all the other Employee tools.** This included performance reviews, quality workshops, diversity training, Seven Habits seminars, and so forth. AMCA Partners made it a priority to attend many of the quarterly business reviews and other TD events. Our goal has been to learn their business, to think and act like an owner, to search for more effective ways to bring in current business opportunities, and to apply the skills of servant leadership to all parts of the business.

12. **TD leaders made servant leadership and business results requirements for employment.** In the mid '90s, we did an audit to make sure all business practices were rewarding a servant-leader's approach. We didn't want to inadvertently confuse Partners by teaching one set of values and practices while business processes rewarded different standards. Meanwhile, Jack Lowe, Jr., and his leadership team drew a line in the sand. From that day forward, every leader within TD would be accountable for both business results and servant leadership. Leaders admitted that previously abusive leadership had been overlooked by some who were good at making the numbers. Going forward, this would no longer be acceptable. If a particular leader was good at one standard, yet rejected, ignored, or simply didn't perform well on the other, then he or she must

either make prompt, significant improvement or find employment elsewhere. It took hard work to make this a reality, but it got the attention of everyone.

13. **A partnership between AMCA and TD's diversity committee created four videos of skits with company Partners that highlighted servant leadership and non-servant leadership behavior in the workplace.** In 1999, a soul-searching session of the TD diversity committee led to an innovation in AMCA's servant leadership classes. The committee found that servant leadership was more "talk than walk" in critical areas of the business. Leaders on the committee openly shared some classic situations when servant leadership was still painfully absent. How could we further strengthen our resolve to put servant leadership into practice in every situation? How could we raise the bar?

In one of TD's regular Friday Forums, founders of the Container Store performed six entertaining skits illustrating their three core values. Even though the skits were "homemade" and somewhat impromptu, the impact was terrific. They inspired us to identify nine typical scenarios showing the gap between our ideal and current practice. We recruited teams of Partners to create fun, quick skits to illustrate the differences. With a small budget and home video equipment, we recruited top leaders to play the roles of leaders stuck in old, abusive styles, which added to the fun. Original music and even dance numbers were created. Don Frick, who had produced TD's 50th anniversary tape, produced nine short videos to be used at job sites as a starting point to stimulate healthy dialogue about what servant leadership is and why it is so important within the culture of TD. The impact of these homemade skits has been felt throughout TD, and they are now available for others to use.

14. **We formed the Servant Leadership Learning Community to consolidate our efforts to help other local organizations wanting to create leaderful cultures (see chapter 7).**

Sometimes people make the mistake of thinking that servant leadership is "soft stuff." Together we have learned that as hard as the technical business challenges are to get right, they are easier than the people side of the equation.

To truly become an effective servant-leader requires courage, persistence, and commitment to the belief that together we can create something more meaningful and successful than we can by working independently.

We salute and thank all our Partners at TD for being patient and inspiring teachers on this journey. We stand in awe of our good fortune to have been at the right place at the right moment. To be given the opportunity to be impacted by the extraordinary lives of Bob Greenleaf and Jack Lowe, Sr., is a rare blessing. Equally, to live within the community of TD Partners over these 30 years has transformed everything about us, from our business vision to our personal commitment to keep growing our servant leadership.

Jack Lowe, Jr., said recently, "After 30 years TD still hasn't produced one perfect servant leader, but a lot of us have become much better leaders." As usual, Jack is disarming with his honesty, humor, and humility. And, of course, he's right. We may never achieve the full measure of what it means to be servant-leaders in every sense of Greenleaf's inspiring vision. Yet Greenleaf challenges us to start within (not outside) on our mission to bring lasting change in the world: **"The servant views any problem in the world as *in here*, inside oneself, not *out there*. And if a flaw in the world is to be remedied, to the servant, the process of change starts *in here*, in the servant, not *out there.*"**

To quote another well-known servant-leader, Mahatma Gandhi, "We must be the change we want to see in the world."

TAKE AWAYS
TO PONDER

1. Greenleaf believed the process of lasting change begins within. What changes are you willing to make to awaken and inspire servant leadership in those around you?

2. We purposely integrated every possible resource, such as a class on diversity and one on Seven Habits by Stephen Covey to strengthen and enrich our work on servant leadership. What resources do you have to draw from in your organization or community?

3. How might you use the 13 descriptions of servant-leaders defined by TD Partners to begin a dialogue within your organization?

4. If you dare to claim bold dreams for your work and life (perhaps taking the next step, if you are already on this journey), how might Greenleaf's essay on *The Servant as Leader* inspire and clarify your direction?

5. We are clear that without the flexibility of each others' unwavering support, we would not have achieved this synergistic progress. Who might you invite into long-term partnership to create a more sustainable and leaderful future together?

CHAPTER

A Force Unleashed:
Engaging Head, Hand, and Heart at the Carrollton Police Department

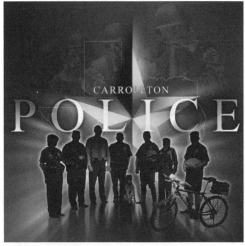

"Success Through Service"

Carrollton, Texas, is a suburb of 115,000 plus citizens in Northwest Dallas. The Carrollton Police Department (CPD) has 161 sworn personnel, 78 civilian personnel, 25 sworn reserve officers, and 40 school crossing guards. Bureaus within the department are Management Services, Investigative Services, and Operations.

Police departments are strictly command-and-control operations. It's always been that way. But in Carrollton, Texas, police have forged a hard-won model of servant leadership that defies traditional definitions. A dramatic example of this involved a team of volunteers that dramatically lowered motor vehicle break-ins in several sectors of the city.

The servant leadership philosophy was first introduced within the CPD by Chief David James, who had read Greenleaf's essay *The Servant as Leader*, which defied the "hero-as-leader" model so popular in America, then and today. In its place, Greenleaf described a leadership path that puts the growth of others ahead of personal ambition for power, rank, or pay. James knew immediately that this was what he believed about leadership.

"Servant leadership is one critical component of an effective management style. It is one thread in the law enforcement tapestry that brings consistency and compassion to bear on everyday citizen concerns," says James.

We have been encouraged by other organizations committed to servant leadership, like TDIndustries and Ann McGee-Cooper & Associates," James continues. "When these two companies organized the Servant Leadership Learning Community (SLLC) in Dallas, we jumped at the opportunity to join."

Chief James has since stepped back to allow Assistant Chief Mac Tristan to represent the police department in the SLLC. For Mac, these quarterly sessions serve to refresh his own commitment as well as connect with other leaders of servant-led organizations in Dallas. Mac always brings an honest disclosure of his own challenges and celebrations. As a result, he has earned the respect and gratitude of everyone in the SLLC.

Mac Tristan

So, the great dream of Robert Greenleaf came to the CPD through David James, then found another servant's heart in Mac Tristan. And Mac didn't hesitate to take what he was learning at the SLLC sessions back to his team.

The police/citizen ratio is about 1/1000, so typical police work is reactive. Officers can spend all their time on "urgent" matters and routine operations ("Driving for Dollars"), never getting around to the important work of solving chronic problems, developing leadership, or practicing the disciplines of a learning organization. Mac wanted to create a new model for policing after years of command-and-control hierarchy.

CPOP Traction

Mac's enthusiasm for empowering officers has inspired a Community Problem-Oriented Policing (CPOP) unit composed of volunteers within the department. CPOP began in May 2004 when Mac invited officers to meet and talk about how they could improve their department as well as their service to the community. His idea was to ignite the passion of these officers by allowing them to act on what they already wanted to do.

Mac also wanted to provide a forum for honest feedback without repercussion, as well as act on urgent crime trends in Carrollton. As a result of his openness and willingness to share power with this group, the officers began to believe in Mac's sincerity, his "walking the talk."

The team's first goal was to communicate more effectively between four sets of 22 patrol officers in different shifts and divisions throughout the CPD. Their second goal was to tackle a tough problem and show the effectiveness of this kind of voluntary servant leadership. The 10 officers on the team ran the meetings, chose the CPOP name and a chairman. They met twice a month, and Mac made sure he missed some of those meetings to send a consistent message that the officers were the decision makers.

Mac handed out some simple guidelines within which these officers were free to make decisions. When considering solutions to any problems, the team must have a consensus in answering yes to each one of these questions:

- Is it ethical?
- Is it legal?
- Is it the right thing for the community?
- Is it the right thing for the CPD?
- Is it within our policies and values?
- Is it something you can take responsibility for and be proud of?

If the team's answer to all of these questions was yes, then it could plan the implementation and do it!

Solving the "Impossible"

The first crime problem the team decided to tackle came in response to an ongoing problem in the community with vehicle break-ins (BMVs).

"What if we could eliminate vehicle break-ins in our community?" Mac asked the team. Some of the officers laughed (not out loud) at this preposterous suggestion. It was an example of a solution that seemed impossible, but Mac believed that it could be accomplished with the collective wisdom of the group and the spirit of servant leadership.

The department was spending 30 hours for each investigation of a BMV and wanted to cut that down drastically. So, they began by targeting the area where most of the break-ins were taking place. This became a significant ingredient in their success. If they had tried to focus on the entire city, they might well have failed.

Then they communicated with neighbors in that part of the community by going door-to-door, leaving fliers when people were not at home. The night shifts reported areas where street lights were out. Street signs were put up advertising the "H.E.A.T." (help end auto theft) effort.

Officers created a report card which they left on car windshields as they walked or biked the beat. The car got a passing grade if it was locked and no valuables were visible within. Conversely, a failing grade was given (and the reason for it) if the car was unlocked or there were valuables visible. Eventually, as the local media caught on and asked what was happening, the CPD got a lot of free publicity to help further their efforts.

Carrollton Policemen at an SLLC Meeting

The results were remarkable. The total number of BMVs reported dropped 94 percent in the first eight months. There were only two BMVs reported in 2006. The team moved into the second and third targeted areas and received no reports of BMVs in the first three months of 2005. There was an 83 percent reduction through mid-2006.

To talk to the officers that pulled off this "impossible" feat is to catch the spirit of servant leadership – to see, feel and hear the passion and energy that is released when those in the best position to effect changes are empowered to do so.

TAKE AWAYS
TO PONDER

1. Assistant Chief Mac Tristan carefully drafted six questions to guide his officers to implement their ideas. What are a few similar guidelines you could draft to free those who report to you to become problem solvers?

2. This leader ignited the creative imagination of his officers by inspiring them to prevent rather than react to problems. How might you recruit volunteers to make a difference by generating and implementing creative solutions to current problems?

3. This leader often did not attend his officer's meetings to keep ownership of their work with them. Are there occasions when your purposeful absence could encourage more positive ownership by others?

CHAPTER

The Tipping Point:
Servant Leadership and
the Parkland Hospital Way

Parkland Health & Hospital System was founded in 1894 with a mandate to furnish medical aid and hospital care to indigent and needy persons residing in Dallas County. It is also the primary teaching hospital for the University of Texas Southwestern Medical Center. With 968 licensed beds, Parkland is the second largest regional Burn Center in the U.S. and the nation's busiest maternity hospital. (16,489 Babies delivered in 2006). Its 6,500 Employees serve the main hospital as well as the nine Community-Oriented Primary Care Health Centers.

If public scandals haven't awakened us to the acute need for servant-leaders today, perhaps the state of health care systems will. Throughout the developed world, health care is in crisis. In America, it has been one of our top domestic challenges for decades. If ever there was a systemic problem that needs a long-term solution, this is it.

Yet, on this very day, you can hear the "faint flutter of wings" of servant leadership within an extraordinary institution in Dallas, Texas: Parkland Health & Hospital System.

Since opening its doors in 1894, Parkland has served the Dallas community, especially those at the lowest economic level. Among recent accolades came this one from a lengthy article in the popular business magazine, *Fast Company:*

"Looking for inspired leadership, passionate employees, unsurpassed productivity, and grateful customers? Forget the dispirited corridors of corporate America. Look instead to the bursting-with-life corridors of Parkland Memorial Hospital, a remarkable place that delivers more than 16,000 babies per year – more babies than any other hospital in the country. That's more babies, in fact, than are born in 10 of America's states. There is still a way for giant organizations to do great work – whatever 'products' they deliver: The Parkland Way." ("Miracle of Birth," in *Fast Company,* October 2002)

Parkland Servant Leadership Class

Toward a Tipping Point

When Dr. Ron Anderson was appointed CEO in 1982, servant leadership found its strongest proponent and voice.

"While there are a lot of changes going on here at Parkland, there are some things that are a part of our culture that we don't want to change. One of the most important is the presence of people who are servant-leaders, who understand what it means to assist and lift up others – patients and their families, but also co-workers."

In 2001, Dr. Anderson asked Jacqualene Stephens, Ph.D., director of Behavioral Health and Social Services, to begin a leadership initiative involving both mentoring and servant leadership. She gathered a servant leadership work team based on recommendations from senior executive staff, who recognized the characteristics of servant leadership in a number of Parkland Employees. The mission of the work team was to read widely, interview leaders at other servant-led institutions, and develop a strategy for Parkland. "They wisely chose to take a patient path toward integrating servant leadership into the fabric of Parkland over the long term." Jacqualene described their strategy,

"We have had many rollouts around a wide variety of culture-changing initiatives, and I knew it would be the kiss of death for servant leadership to become just another rollout. Instead, we are using a model proposed in *The Tipping Point,* in which change is brought about by gaining a critical mass of people to support it. At that point, even a large system can be tipped in favor of the change desired. We are engaging people primarily by piquing their curiosity about servant leadership."

Jacqualene Stephens

Parkland Mandate, Mission, Vision, and Guiding Principles

Circles of Life

Mandate

To furnish medical aid and hospital care to indigent and needy persons residing in the hospital district.

Compassion – We will provide service in a spirit of empathy, love, and concern.

Integrity – We will be honest, trustworthy, authentic, humble, and transparent in all our relationships. We will demonstrate devotion to duty and to the service of others.

Mission

Dedicated to the health and well being of individuals and communities entrusted to our care.

Respect – We will treat everyone fairly in recognition of their intrinsic worth.

Vision

By our actions, we will define the standards of excellence for public academic health systems.

Collaboration – We will work together with our patients and partners.

Leadership – We will create a servant-led environment.

Guiding Principle

Our values and principles reflect our shared responsibility to achieve health care excellence for our patients and communities.

Excellence – We will provide high standards of service and performance.

Stewardship – We will manage resources responsibly and bring value to patients and taxpayers.

As a part of this strategy, Parkland joined the Dallas-based Servant Leadership Learning Community (SLLC), an 11-member consortium dedicated to developing "leaderful" cultures within the context of a learning community (further described in chapter 7). Parkland then asked Ann McGee-Cooper & Associates (AMCA), the host of the SLLC, to help design a curriculum of servant leadership. Two daylong sessions were held, in which both positional and opinion leaders were invited to help shape the course. In 2003, a health care grant from the state of Texas through the Bill Priest Institute (part of the Dallas County Community College District) allowed Parkland and AMCA to design a series of three all-day classes on servant leadership for Parkland Employees. About 60 Employees attended the classes and were then invited to participate in an internal learning community monthly gathering to extend the learning from these classes back into the culture.

Parkland Servant Leadership Class

Called to Serve

One of the learning modules from the servant leadership classes focuses on "Work as Calling," in which participants tell their stories of why they choose to serve at Parkland. An example of their heartfelt desire to help others less fortunate was shared by Karen Mulloney, past Director, Community and Corporate Fundraising, Parkland Foundation:

During my first holiday season at Parkland, a gentleman appeared at my office door. He was dressed in clean but very tattered clothes, and I quickly determined that he was in the wrong place. As I started to escort him to Social Services, he asked me if I was the Money Lady. My response was "Yes," as we both settled into chairs to continue our conversation. He then told me a story that has made a profound impact on my life.

Karen Mulloney

He held his closed fist out and as he opened it, dropped something into my hand. He said, "It takes me the entire year to save this money, but I want to help those less fortunate." In my hand was a neatly folded $50 bill. As I fought to maintain my composure, I thanked him and asked for his address so that we could send him an acknowledgment letter. He then told me he was being evicted at the end of the month and that he would probably not receive his mail. I walked with him to the exit and listened as he told me that Parkland had been so helpful to him and he felt blessed to be able to help others.

I think of this gentleman often and say a prayer of thanks that we met. He is a constant reminder for me to never judge a person on outward appearances. He is what Parkland is all about ... a belief in the worth of each individual and a genuine desire to assist those less fortunate.

Servant leadership classes continued in 2004 and 2005, amid public controversy surrounding the expansion of Parkland, the continuing and intense budget crisis, loss of more than 500 staff, and a facility that is 54 percent over capacity for what the hospital is trying to provide for Dallas County.

Meanwhile, Jacqualene Stephens, Linda Wilkerson, and the servant leadership work team started their own internal SLLC for Employees who had participated in the classes. They began meeting quarterly to continue learning about and applying servant leadership to their work at Parkland.

In 2006 and 2007, we continued the journey, hoping to reach that tipping point that will enable virtually anyone at Parkland to sense the spirit of servant leadership in action. A very successful presentation at the Leadership Forum and new executive leaders who embrace servant leadership have given new hope in the midst of very trying circumstances.

> "Let us not look for the door and the way out anywhere but in the wall against which we are living. Let us seek the respite where it is – in the very thick of battle."
>
> Albert Camus

The dozens of servant-leaders within Parkland can take courage that their ordinary, daily work of service to others is not in vain.

Dr. Anderson comments: "We must remain vigilant and be sure to place proper value on maintaining our capability and capacity to serve. We need to do this in a humane fashion that also pays attention not only to outcomes, but also to amenities and the creation of a healing environment. The future is an exciting time that we must prepare for. Gandhi said, 'We must become the change that we seek in the world.' Our task is to continue in the spirit of servant leadership and sound stewardship to be that agent of change and champion for the health of our community. To do that we will need, and ask for, unwavering support."

Dr. Ron Anderson

TAKE AWAYS
TO PONDER

1. Big, high-profile rollouts of new cultural initiatives often fade away within a year or two. How might you learn from *The Tipping Point* strategy, which encourages volunteers and trusted opinion leaders to become owners and ambassadors for healthy change?

2. The leadership initiative purposely built on the culture of inspiring personal dedication that had been part of Parkland's tradition since their beginning. What positive attributes can you find in your organization to help you grow a strong culture of trust based on that positive foundation?

3. Daring to live a life of calling has become a compelling theme at Parkland. How might your life change if you chose to live according to your sacred calling?

CHAPTER

Celebration Restaurant:
A Feast of Food, Family, and
Servant Leadership

Celebration Restaurant opened in March 1971 to bring people of all ages and cultures together to eat good food in a natural setting. Two old houses, a full-service bar and patio, complete with a stone fireplace and fountain, have since been added. In 1994, a catering business began and now serves breakfast or lunch to 250 companies, as well as handling special events, receptions, bar mitzvahs, and other social gatherings. Celebration Market opened next to the restaurant in 2000 to serve Customers who prefer to eat in the comfort of their own homes.

At a Servant Leadership Learning Community (SLLC) session hosted by Celebration, Ed Lowe, owner of the restaurant, sat with five of his partners: Chuck Girard, John Stout, Megan Lintner, Gerald Johnson, and Elizabeth Mata. One by one, they told their stories.

Ed told how his father, Jack Lowe, Sr., believed in him when he was a young man, struggling with what to do with his life. He had dropped out of college and was working as a leather craftsman. Then, he got an idea to start a restaurant and leather shop as a way to earn a living. His dad had borrowed a small amount of money from an aunt to start the business that became TDIndustries. So Ed asked to borrow some money to start the business he envisioned, which became Celebration Restaurant.

Celebration...
then and now

Ed explained that most everyone thought it was a crazy idea that would never work. Perhaps even his dad doubted, yet he stood behind Ed all the way. This gave Ed the strength and determination to want to prove them all wrong. And, in time, he has. Celebration Restaurant now stands as one of the most unique family restaurants in Dallas, known for excellent food and memorable Customer service.

Ed's Journey

Describing his journey to become a servant-leader, Ed explained, "Several things have happened that have changed me as a leader. The first was to discover that I was more like my mom than my dad. My mom is a great woman who gets lots done, yet she can be bossy – and so can I. My dad, on the other hand, knew how to step back and give others room to lead.

"Not so long ago I learned that we had made lots of mistakes with a big Customer in our catering business. We met with the Customer and identified the problems. We then formed a leadership team to develop a strategy. The most important component of the plan was to have a kitchen staff meeting to brainstorm solutions and get everyone onboard with solving the problems. Kitchen staff meetings had historically been John Stout and me with a long agenda and a translator to present our ideas to a roomful of Spanish-speaking Partners. The staff would sit with a 'when will this be over' look on their face and offer very little of their vast knowledge of how things worked in our kitchen. Our team agreed that without the staff's ideas and buy-in that we could never achieve our goals.

"We then decided that our bilingual team members, Adan Flores, Salvador Jimenez, and Elizabeth Mata, should plan and conduct the staff meeting. The difference was dramatic. Everyone understood how important it was to all of us to keep this Customer. There was great energy and engaging dialogue. They agreed on solutions to address the previous problems.

"I'm certain that the key to saving the Customer was to give up control and use a team approach allowing the bilingual leadership with the staff to plan and execute solutions."

"I also decided to start working at 4:00 A.M., to pitch in and ensure that we executed our new plan. I was amazed that our staff worked straight through, without breaks, to get this huge job out on time. Nobody stopped to eat or to rest until the early afternoon. Some even went out to work evening caterings. We worked 8 consecutive 12-hour shifts beginning at 4:00 A.M. During this time, no one ever complained of being tired. I knew these folks were hard workers, but during this time working together I gained not only an appreciation for how hard they worked, but what fine people they were. Not only did we keep the Customer and earn several new Customers from our improved performance, but also an enormous amount of trust and friendship was built. I began to rethink my role as leader and decided to work much harder at becoming a better servant-leader."

Partner's Pride

John Stout has been Ed's partner for 30 years. He manages the kitchen and considers his main work keeping morale high and ensuring an excellent product every day. "This is truly a leaderful company," he reflected. "Ed and I have worked together so long. I love him like a brother. We have our differences, but we always work them out. The best interest of our Employees, our Customers, and the success of Celebration is what matters most to us."

Megan Lintner has transformed Celebration's catering business, bringing enormous entrepreneurial creativity and energy. This is not only vital for profitability, it has also expanded career opportunities for their team. She came to Celebration from the corporate world, where the pyramid of power determined most everything. She comments:

"Here, power flows both ways," she commented on the difference at Celebration. "The commitment to grow people here, promoting from within, is a big contrast to the mentality in the corporate world."

We share information to increase the sense of shared ownership of this business and to ensure accountability."

Gerald Johnson told a story of what it was like to be in this incredible "family." He recounted that when his father was very ill, Ed and the entire team stood behind him as he took extra time to support his dad. Choking back tears, Gerald shared how much it meant when life throws you a curve and all your business partners rise up to help you through the hard times. Others joined in, saying it was really fun to come to work. The group's strong friendships made the work they did together truly enjoyable.

Ed Lowe and Gerald Johnson

Then, Elizabeth Mata told her story. She began work at Celebration as a vegetable cutter in the kitchen speaking no English. One day she was asked if she would like to drive the catering truck out to jobs. She only knew the way to and from work, so she expressed fear that she would get lost.

"No problem," she was told by her supervisor. "I'll go with you and show you the way!" So the two drove to Fort Worth, an hour away from Dallas. "Then it was my turn to drive it alone," Elizabeth said. "I was scared, but I did it."

"I was also scared because I was able to speak very few words of English," she confided. "They told me to just smile and say yes to whatever I was told. Somehow, I was successful. But I came to Ed and told him I wanted to learn English. He paid my tuition to attend classes at El Centro Community College, where I increased my English skills."

Elizabeth Mata

Ed then informed us that Elizabeth went on to become a captain in their catering business, taking teams out and serving large parties in grand style. She not only conquered her fears and became a sterling example of what can happen when you are willing to learn and grow, she now helps everyone around her learn what she has been taught in the business. "If I can do it, you can too!" she encourages with a convincing smile.

Ed gave generous credit to Elizabeth and his team for helping him learn what it means to become a servant-leader. It means leading through mutual trust instead of coercive power. It means relying on Employees to help find the answers. It means trusting that others want to do good work. It means deeply caring about each other and finding better solutions together. It means creating a great place to work where everyone feels encouraged to contribute. It means becoming leaderful.

Chuck Girard was the general manager at Celebration at the time of our SLLC session. "Because learning to speak English was such an important business tool and was limiting so many of our Employees, the restaurant decided to buy several computers for use in the homes of Employees who wanted this opportunity." They bought Rosetta Stone software, which teaches English as a second language. Partners could pay the company back for the computers a small amount each month.

What is happening is amazing. Families are learning English together. Those who were formerly limited to working in the kitchen or busing tables could now become waiters, making more money. Even more important, learning to speak English opens many doors in every aspect of life.

Dreams Fulfilled

Then, Ed told of one of his dreams. He has always loved nature, and for years, he has taken youngsters on canoe trips down the Brazos River. In 2005, he formed a group called "Friends of the Brazos" to raise awareness that the river was in trouble. So much Brazos water was being sold to large industrial interests that the river ecosystem was dying. Several times a year Ed takes groups of young people on canoe trips to introduce them to nature and raise their awareness that we all must take an active role in preserving and protecting our environment.

Ed Lowe with Friends of the Brazos

"I couldn't do these trips that are so important to me if I didn't have all these great people keeping our business alive in my absence. They have taught me priceless gifts of servant leadership. Each of them are leaders in our business. And each of them are teaching other Partners our values and our business. It began with my dad's unconditional love and trust in me as a young man searching for my life's work. Together, we have all grown into that trust and created something that continues to surprise us all."

Finally, a new tradition is growing at Celebration Restaurant. Ed has been sponsoring Dinner with Dialogue, reserving a place within the restaurant for guest speakers to talk about community issues. After a brief presentation, the floor is opened to dialogue. So far, topics have included ways to strengthen our public schools; a dialogue on competing concerns of Hispanics, African Americans, and Anglos; and understanding how microlending lifts millions of women and their families out of poverty.

What began as a way for a few young hippies to support themselves is now a thriving gathering place where servant leadership benefits all who come to enjoy good food, extraordinary service, and good fellowship.

TAKE AWAYS
TO PONDER

1. When Celebration Restaurant owner Ed Lowe spent time working with his front-line Employees, he realized how dedicated they were, beginning early in the morning until late at night, and how much he had underestimated their commitment. When was the last time you joined workers on the front lines of your organization to experience firsthand, what they experience every day? Why not plan this into your schedule?

2. When Elizabeth Mata was entrusted with more than she thought she was capable of, she rose to the challenge, learned new parts of the business, and became a teacher of others. Who might you be overlooking in your organization – someone who might respond to a new challenge?

3. Ed saw the need for ESL education among many of his Employees and provided a training method and equipment to help them learn English. What kind of training might make a big difference to your Employees? How might you provide it?

4. When Ed realized that his Hispanic Employees were not interacting during meetings, he turned meetings over to someone who could engage them in Spanish and English and got much more ownership. When was the last time you delegated the responsibility to lead a meeting to someone else? Who would be a good candidate?

5. Dinner with Dialogue encourages conversations about community issues challenging our lives. Are there ways you might initiate dialogue to help people come together and listen with open minds and hearts while expanding the pool of shared meaning?

CEO Steve Saunders and the Tempo team

CHAPTER

Son of Servant Leadership:
The Tempo Mechanical Story

Tempo Mechanical is an Employee-owned company whose goal is to be the premier provider of residential mechanical services for North Texas. A spinoff of TDIndustries in 1998, Tempo adopted its parent company's servant leadership culture and has won many awards: National Residential Contractor of the Year; one of the six "Best Companies to Work For" in our industry (Air Conditioning Heating and Refrigeration NEWS); *recipient of the "National Carrier Distinguished Dealer" award (1996) for outstanding business processes and high levels of Customer satisfaction.*

It began on August 15, 1997, with these fateful words: "Steve," Jack Lowe said, "before we begin your quarterly business review, Ben and I want to tell you that we have completed the strategic planning process and decided that your division is not strategic."

In his heart, Steve Saunders had known the answer months before they did, but was not yet ready to accept it. Now, like it or not, the Tempo team was leaving TDIndustries. Steve realized, "We could create our own future, or let the future dictate to us."

The discussion was clean, clear, and simple. "TDIndustries can fire you all or sell you, or you can buy yourself. You won't be here in one year," Jack said in his typical, respectful, yet honest tone of voice.

The Spinoff

Here was the analysis: Tempo was a $9 million residential A/C, heating business, mildly profitable, with about 2500 square feet of office space and 5000 square feet of warehouse. The division created havoc at TD because of the radically different needs from the Mechanical Installation System and a Customer base that had requirements for additional infrastructure and overhead. With Tempo gone, TD could spend much less to expand and delay expensive capital improvements for building expansion. Still, it was more a strategic decision than a financial decision for TD.

In typical TD fashion, Jack and Ben told Steve, "We're not going to sell Tempo to the highest priced offer. Our goal is to put the Tempo Partners in the best possible position for long-term success."

"Still, they thought they were throwing us to the wolves," Steve recalls. "But, they left the choice of our future to us, and we had options to consider."

The consolidation movement was gaining momentum in the air-conditioning industry, and early on that seemed like the smartest strategy. Yet, over time, a growing consensus developed among the Tempo Partners that they did not want to find outside owners.

Steve Saunders

"We want to buy ourselves," they said. And, after extensive work in teams and small groups, collectively they agreed to build a company like the one they were leaving. The fundamental tenets of the new company would be *Employee Ownership, Servant Leadership,* and *Performance Excellence,* later recognized as the three gifts of their heritage.

The seven-person Tempo leadership team worked on addressing the current value of the company. At a strategy meeting, they agreed on a potential purchase offer. "One million five. Not a penny more. That's fair."

The vote to self-purchase was unanimous.

In an amazing coincidence, not more than a minute after that vote, TD CEO Jack Lowe entered the lobby of the newly rented Tempo facility. Jack had two moldy AC grills in his hands and wanted them cleaned and painted. "We'll get you some new grills," Steve told him. "You don't need to be back on that ladder anyway. Now, come on in and let's talk. You're timing is perfect. We want to buy ourselves."

Jack perked up and smiled. "I'm so glad you said that. I've been thinking about how you could buy it." He went up to the board and began drawing up his vision of fair value, hard assets, and exact replacement costs. Before the hour was out, a basic agreement was completed.

The transition wasn't easy. There were legal details, operational strategy, and organizational development, along with the purchase of new accounting, estimating, and software systems. The ESOP (internal Partner stockholder plan) transfer was a legal nightmare. Tempo also needed to buy the business assets and ongoing contracts, which TD agreed to sell.

In addition, the group had no operating capital. A suggestion was made to approach suppliers and ask if they would extend credit terms from 30 to 60 days. Both major suppliers, Comfort Supply and Carrier-Bock agreed, telling Tempo, "We believe in you." Shortly thereafter, the company also got a line of credit from a major bank.

The spinoff date came and went as planned. And, when the ESOP investment window closed, Tempo Partners invested one million dollars of their TD stock, their 401k's, and even cash contributions. The amount came as a staggering surprise to those on the outside. Tempo was off and running. Even more amazing, the basic capital structure was more solid than most in the industry.

TD's strategic decision now seemed prescient as well as compassionate. The transition was made when the building market was red hot. The business environment was healthy, and the rising tide lifted Tempo's boat along with the market. Good leadership, careful money management, and the ESOP contributions created the best possible outcome for the Partners of both companies. The transition point of this venture came on June 12, 1999, when Tempo gave TD the last check of the money owed to complete the purchase of the business. Before the end of the first year, Tempo was debt free!

The three gifts of Tempo's heritage would each be crucial to the creation and sustenance of the business during the challenging times to come. *Employee Ownership* created the capital base that allowed for debt-free operation. *Servant Leadership* built the trust between Tempo and its suppliers and bankers that produced the initial operating capital and line of credit. And, *Performance Excellence* allowed the team to quickly develop the strategies, processes, and procedures to solve the problems of transition in a rapidly growing business opportunity. Had they not had all three gifts, they might easily have sunk.

Boom and Bust

The summer of '98 brought a booming building market and the hottest weather since 1980. Steve recalls, "On June 1, we were confronted with 86 jobs scheduled and a capacity to do only one-half of that. We spent the entire month of June trying to get builders to take back work."

During this time, the first seeds of what Saunders calls "the great schism" were sown. "We looked at each other and determined never to let the business get out of control again. We worked intensely hard at building systems and processes to predict, plan, schedule work, do work, and be a much better contractor."

One of the ways they did this was to commit to the Baldrige quality process. Steve, who was a Texas Quality Award examiner in his TD days, pulled out the Baldrige book, hired some consultants to help guide the process at Tempo, and applied for the Texas Award for Performance Excellence. To the delight of Tempo Partners, they received a site visit. The first day went smoothly. On day two, though, the answers didn't come as easily. There were questions about integration, deployment, process, and linkage. Tempo leaders knew that they had come close, but Tempo wasn't ready for such a prestigious award. Victory, however, was in the preparation.

The process of getting ready for Baldrige fundamentally set Tempo apart in early 2000, and the company rode on that effort for several years. But, a significant part of the management team burned out. Saunders could envision the team as highly profitable and painted that vision for Partners, yet when it didn't come quickly, they were disappointed.

In fall of 2001, business slowed radically. A work backlog of over 3.6 million dollars quickly dropped to 1.8 million. At the same time, Tempo was moving into another building, which had been purchased and renovated using the line of credit. After the 9/11 attacks, new business orders literally stopped. In addition, one builder sent a letter stating, "We can't pay the $750,000 we owe you. We won't ever be able to pay you and hope that this doesn't hurt you."

At this critical pressure point, there were two options: lay off one-third of the company, or pressure the builder to pay up. "We got paid every dime and kept the Customer," recalled Saunders. He attributes the success to servant leadership, but also to threats to take that business into bankruptcy if they didn't work it out. Even though that builder eventually went out of business, Tempo now works for three out of four of the companies its leaders joined, which has accounted for millions in current revenue. The close relationships developed during that trying time paid off. The power of relationships, ethical business dealings, and direct communication each played a role in the successful recouping of the money. Fortunately for Tempo, in the first few days of January 2002, purchase orders started flying out of the fax machine. "Had we terminated one-third of our workforce, we couldn't have kept up with the volume. It was a scary and painful time," Saunders says.

The next few years were tough. Tempo earned mild profits that mostly benefited the ESOP. Partners who had worked hard just to get to this point now were faced with rough waters ahead and the prospects of low profitability. Builders were mean, hard, and scared, taking the lowest price. Tempo rolled with the punches and figured out how to grow an energy consulting business called TexEnergy Solutions. Good profits were on the horizon.

The Great Schism

But patience wasn't shared by all. Many of those who had worked so hard were ready for a share of the rewards of their investment in the company. When they were told there wasn't any way to do that yet, the response was that Tempo needed to go in a different direction. Translation: the CEO needed to go.

The lines were drawn in 2004. Steve remained hopeful that they could recapture the same enthusiasm, teamwork, affection, and love that had launched the company. Instead, all they did was fight. Plot. Not talk to each other. Undercut each other. There were no good or bad people in the fight, just a lot of frustration that boiled over. Some were frustrated with TDIndustries' servant leadership community investment model. It seemed too slow, too hard. The local economy was in a recession, but they didn't see that as relevant.

During that frustrating year, loyalties were divided. Gossip and stonewalling ran rampant. There was internal theft. It got bloody, ugly, just plain bad. When the final numbers came in for the first half of 2004, Tempo was deep in the hole – $300,000 in the red, in violation of bank covenants, and $200,000 in inventory missing, plus another $150,000 loss that Tempo Partners didn't know about at the time. "We had a come to Jesus meeting, and it was not a fun time," recalls Steve. The disaffected group wanted to get rid of the CEO, thinking that would solve Tempo's problems. And without a plan for immediate business success, Steve kept asking himself whether he was the problem.

The leaders at Tempo left that tense Tuesday morning meeting in factions. They agreed that each group would firm up a plan and present it on Friday. The disaffected ones immediately began soliciting board members to get rid of Steve. Board members came to Steve and reported the lobbying that was going on, so he was aware of what the others were doing. They were making commitments and trying to build an alternative consensus.

"My servant leadership challenge was to play fair. I had the right to terminate them. I had the technical right as trustee of ESOP to vote the shares. But I wasn't going to lobby the board members, and I was not going to violate our one-share, one-vote agreement. I figured the board knew what they had in me and it would have to decide what solution was best," Steve remembers.

By Friday, Steve knew he had the votes. He also knew that there would be no "let's work out a plan together." Only winners and losers. On Friday morning, the 14 Strategic Planning Team members met. The leader of Steve's opposition made an impassioned plea, stating in no uncertain terms, "This company is not big enough for the two of us." It was a "Showdown at the OK Corral." There were two plans to vote on. Steve Saunders and Tempo going forward, or Tempo without Steve. The vote was 6 to 3 in favor of the historical strategy.

Steve looked at one of the disaffected leaders and said, "Looks like you can resign or I can fire you. Which would you prefer?" "I quit." "Thank you," Steve said.

But, he just sat there, so I told him he could leave now. He teared up as it hit him that he was suddenly without a job. He'd given so much. He had been a big contributor. But he got lost in his perception that he was the key leader of Tempo. Ironically, the very confidence that made him an effective leader now sabotaged him.

Steve turned to the second leader. "I resign," she said, "but want to help you work through the transition." The third person wanted to get back with Steve on a decision.

"I wish all those people well," Steve reflected more than two years later. "We won't be friends like in the past. But we eventually bought their stock back and worked hard to do it sooner, rather than later. We had to operate with less, but it was fairer to pay them back their shares.

"It was a horrible year. I had to will myself to come to work every day. Servant leadership had to be my vision if it was going to be my Partners' vision; my hope had to be visible for them to hope; my efforts had to be there for them to exert an effort. If I gave up, it was over. I never pretended it was anything but 'let's knock it out one piece at a time.' I thought it was possible to succeed, but I wasn't sure how big the hole was."

Today, Tempo is a dramatically better-managed company. The kinds of opportunities that Tempo envisioned are now coming to fruition. A 9 million-dollar company in 1998, Tempo was a 26 million-dollar company in 2006. Momentum has returned, as has systems analysis. The crisis in leadership created clarity. The trust built among the Partner group allowed Tempo to quickly reorganize and function with a dramatically lower overhead. Tempo became a team again, an extended family working together and held together by the three gifts of its heritage – Employee Ownership, Servant Leadership, and Performance Excellence. These three gifts have repeatedly been fundamental to survival and success.

TAKE AWAYS
TO PONDER

1. Steve Saunders faced one of the most difficult work challenges: what to do when your services are no longer wanted. He found the courage to put the future of his Partners first and persevered to create positive options even when there appeared to be none. How are you "acting like an owner" now, to prepare for such a possibility? Do you have a backup plan?

2. Strife among Employees and hostility toward the CEO nearly derailed Tempo. Steve chose to believe there were not good or bad people; rather, there were strong differences of opinion. How can respect for adversaries open new possibilities for win-win solutions in your organization? How do you handle internal strife in your organization, especially when you are involved? What preventive measures might you adopt now?

3. After the board voted to keep Steve on as CEO, he had to keep the vision of servant leadership in front of him at all times and will himself to come to work every day. What challenges in your work call for both fierce resolve and humility? How do you maintain the tension between the two?

CHAPTER

The Power of LUV:
An Inside Peek at the Innovative Culture Committee of Southwest Airlines

Southwest Airlines (SWA) has long been known for setting and achieving incredible records of performance in their industry. Recognized as #1 and #2 by Fortune *magazine's "100 Best Companies to Work for in America," Southwest has been consistently profitable every quarter for 34 years. The Company's net income for 2006 was $499 million, with 96.4 million Customers and over 32,000 Employees. Southwest is the only airline to win the Triple Crown (#1 in most on-time flights, least lost baggage, and fewest Customer complaints) for five years in a row. How is Southwest able to sustain its unmatched record? Southwest would tell you it's the magic of its People. "If the greatness of a Company is measured by the hearts and souls of its People, then we are indeed the richest Company in the world," says Colleen Barrett, President of SWA. Colleen's own servant leadership can clearly be seen inside the amazing Culture Committee of Southwest Airlines, one of her many innovations that nurtures hearts and minds and keeps SOUTHWEST SPIRIT thriving.*

S o what is the secret, the DNA, of this legendary company so well-known for Positively Outrageous Service, the industry's best record of profitability, and ranked by its Employees as one of the best places to work in America? Many would credit its culture, which the Company defines as:

- Warrior Spirit
- Leading with a Servant's Heart
- and a Fun-LUVing Attitude!

These are the hallmarks SWA works hard to keep alive in the hearts, minds, and daily actions of every Employee.

But there's more to the story. Herb Kelleher, the chairman of the board, and Colleen Barrett, president, are both important catalysts. Yet with 32,000 people, the culture has to go beyond two Leaders, and they would be the first to insist that it does. Indeed, there are countless noteworthy contributors, but one – the Culture Committee – is the foundation from which so much originates.

The Queen of Culture

You can't really understand the Culture Committee without understanding Colleen Barrett, often referred to as "Corporate Mom." Colleen inspires the vision, empowers Employees at every level to become a family, models the way of servant leadership, and gives abundant recognition to others, encouraging the hearts of 32,000 Southwest Employees.

Colleen joined Herb as his legal secretary in 1967. She discovered that Herb worked out of two offices, one to meet with clients and the other a room piled high with papers. Herb went on vacation shortly after hiring Colleen, and she went to work organizing all his loose papers into labeled folders. A Senior Partner in Herb's law firm walked by the office as she worked and was aghast. "Who are you and what are you doing?" he asked with alarm. "I'm Herb's new secretary and I'm organizing his papers,"

Colleen Barrett

58

Colleen replied. "You can't do that! He won't be able to find a thing. Why, he'll fire you!" he exclaimed. "He can't if he wants to be able to find things!" she replied confidently. And she was right. Herb took Colleen everywhere after that and she has been his partner and understudy ever since.

Colleen earned a two-year associate's degree and then demonstrated the capacity to keep learning from all those around her, integrating their knowledge with her own remarkable qualities. First, she always looks for what needs to be done and takes ownership. But she also brings humility and a big heart to her work. Early in the history of SWA when the Company was struggling to stay alive financially, Colleen brought up the future of the People, and Herb gave her responsibility for the People Department and Customers. She has contributed remarkable vision, innovation and servant leadership to both.

One hallmark of Colleen's genius is finding creative ways to honor People on a very sparse budget. Colleen is known internally for her "Bible," a growing list of words, terms, and writing guidelines approved by Colleen for internal and external documents. This includes correct spelling, punctuation, and words to capitalize, such as People, Employee, Customer, Leader, and Company when referring to SWA. She discovered this was a great way to show respect while not costing a penny.

Southwest Airlines' Halloween Celebration

As the Company kept doubling in size, Colleen, then Executive VP of Customers, formed the Culture Committee. At first, it was made up of approximately 38 opinion leaders from all levels and departments of SWA, each of whom was handpicked as exemplifying SOUTHWEST SPIRIT. I (Ann) was lucky enough to be invited to join this group, the result of a letter I wrote suggesting ways to improve Southwest's image from a Customer's perspective. I asked to come inside the Company to learn all I could about what makes it so unique. Today, the Culture Committee is a vibrant team of 120 dedicated Employees – the lifeblood and heartbeat of the Spirit of Southwest Airlines.

The Culture Committee's mission:

To help create the SOUTHWEST SPIRIT and Culture where needed; to enrich it and make it better where it already exists; and to liven it up in places where it might be floundering. In short, this group's goal is to do "WHATEVER IT TAKES" to create, enhance, and enrich the special SOUTHWEST SPIRIT and Culture that has made this such a wonderful Company/Family.

Each member who serves on the Culture Committee does so as a volunteer. We all commit to four all-day meetings once a quarter. For most, this also includes the time required to travel to and from the Dallas Headquarters, so it is no small effort. In addition, we commit to participate in at least three Spirit events each year, and most members pitch in to help with many more. From the beginning, I was tremendously impressed that attendance was 100 percent, and everyone delivered on their promises. I had never served on a committee with such high accountability.

I soon learned that holding people accountable is another of Colleen's unique traits. A member who fails to attend without a valid reason is politely replaced, no hard feelings. When the first members rotated off after three years of service, they collectively declared themselves Alumni Members and stayed active in support of Culture Committee initiatives. This has been the tradition ever since. I find this extraordinary, and yet this is the fabric that keeps SWA so strong – another example of leading with a servant's heart!

None of these initiatives came from MBA graduates or other traditional sources. An important aspect of SWA is that it grew out of the instincts of its Leaders, approximately 40 percent female and 30 percent minority. Below are some of the qualities Colleen has woven into the Culture Committee that have produced incredible results. Note that all of these qualities are also characteristics of servant leadership.

A few Fun-LUVing 2006 Culture Committee Members

Qualities of SWA Culture

Leading with a servant's heart. Colleen, known as the mother of Southwest, works passionately to lift up others and grow their skills. She holds herself and others accountable, and she's there in the hour of need. In short, Colleen has always strived to model the selfless spirit of service that she believes so fervently grows a strong, unmatched culture of service. She encourages all others to care for their station or department Employees with the same loving spirit.

Be the change you want to see in others. Colleen cites the Golden Rule, "Treat others as you want to be treated." "It is so simple," she says. From the beginning, Herb and Colleen knew that for Employees to deliver what they describe as Positively Outrageous Customer Service, Employees had to experience this same loving spirit and generous support from their leaders and their colleagues.

Customers come second. From the beginning, this principle has been an important part of the uniqueness of SWA. Herb and Colleen were clear that Employees could only serve their Customers with exemplary and memorable Customer service if Employees were confident they were supported in the same way. They reasoned that the Customer is not always right. In some cases, a Customer can be abusive. In those situations, Leaders have politely but firmly stood behind their Employees, asking abusive Customers to take their business elsewhere.

Colleen sees this as applying the Golden Rule. If Employees know they will be supported if they err and are leaning toward the Customer, they are more likely to make on-the-spot creative decisions to solve problems and delight their Customers.

Case in point: A Gate Agent told the story of a Customer breaking her leg when she slipped on the ramp while boarding a flight. It was late at night and the Gate Agent leased a private plane to fly the Customer to emergency medical care. This Employee was supported and honored by her Leaders for exemplary Customer service!

Another inspiring example is the story of the Customer Service Agent in Baltimore/Washington who was still in her probationary period. When a late flight from BWI to Long Island, New York, was cancelled due to weather, the agent hired three buses to get her Customers safely to their destination that evening. She was commended by her Leaders.

These examples illustrate the trust Leaders have in their Employees to do the right thing, and the authority they give Employees to act. This is a hallmark of servant leadership in action.

Deep listening with no agenda. When I asked Joyce Rogge, retired Senior VP of Marketing, why Colleen and the Culture Committee have been so successful, she cited Colleen's unique gift to listen very intently with no agenda. So much of each Culture Committee meeting is about listening to the members (now grown to 120 People, plus many alumni). "What problems do we need to address this year?" Might be an opening topic. With representatives from all 63 stations and all parts of the airline present, Colleen can quickly take the pulse of the business. Top Leaders always participate, so this has been an extremely effective way to identify challenges early and get at them proactively before they gain momentum.

Follow up. Don't ask if you are not going to act on what you learn. Joyce Rogge shared another observation about her mentor, Colleen. Colleen has earned huge trust from being reliably consistent in her follow-through. She can be surprisingly generous in her support for what may seem like small ideas. Equally, she can be tenacious, listening to get to the root of complex problems. Recently Southwest conducted a thorough Employee Satisfaction Survey. With support from her leadership team, Colleen formed cross-functional teams to address and report back on each issue. The results of the survey are shared monthly in LUV LINES, the internal Company newsletter, with Colleen addressing each major issue, point by point. Her bottom-up strategy is to address every concern with such integrity that when the next survey comes along in two years, the percentage of responses will be even higher. More Employees will trust that this is a safe way to provide honest feedback and all will know if the solutions are working. Colleen is endeavoring to ensure it is safe to be 100 percent open and honest when responding to the Employee Survey. She believes that trust must be earned on a daily basis. This is another tenet of Southwest Culture and Leadership.

Seeing things whole. Gathering people on all sides of an issue to explore solutions. Some years ago, Flight Attendants, Pilots, and Crew Schedulers were polarized. It's not fun to be the person calling others back to work when someone is ill and needs a substitute. Nor is it welcomed to have your personal plans suddenly interrupted if you are crew. Rancor was brewing. Colleen quickly formed a team of people on all sides and charged them with coming up with solutions. A big part of the team's solution was to bring empathy and appreciation to each other's positions by changing places. With some creative education and leading with a servant's heart, this problem became an opportunity to go the extra mile for a colleague needing help!

Heroes of the Heart Celebration 2006

Constantly teaching the complexities of the business. There is no better champion of this than Tonda Montague, Senior Director, Employee Communications, whose team creates LUV LINES, the award-winning internal newsletter. Tonda and her team create games, charts, and endless ways to draw readers into understanding the complex facts of their business. This includes a mock scandal sheet called "Plane Tales," and "Coloring Outside the Lines," a fun directory of Leaders pictured as little kids, providing lots of fun, personal facts such as nicknames in grade school. Some years ago they worked to raise awareness of how small acts contribute to very large results. For example, they showed the interior of one of Southwest's planes filled with bags of peanuts, with the caption, "We could buy 2.2 million bags of peanuts with what we pay for one day of health care. The plane fact: health care costs are attacking Southwest." That same year they changed their policy to trust their Employee's word when he or she took sick days rather than requiring a doctor's note. This simple decision has saved huge amounts of money each year since.

On Valentine's Day 2007, Southwest celebrated their 16th annual Heroes of the Heart event. Yet another innovation from the Culture Committee, this is a time each year when a group of unsung heroes, those who work hard behind the scenes, are surprised and honored as the Heroes of our Heart. This year, the Internal Customer Care Department was chosen, a group of seven women who make sure that every special event in the lives of 32,000 Employees is appropriately honored and recognized. Among other things, this group has sent special care packages to all those in the military serving our country abroad. The Customer Care Department name flies on a special SWA plane for one year in the group's honor.

This year Herb Kelleher made a surprise tribute naming Colleen Heroine of the Heart, with her special insignia painted on a Southwest Airlines jet to fly in her honor for a year. The tribute reads:

Colleen Barrett

This Southwest Airlines jet
Is dedicated on Valentine's Day 2007 to
Colleen C. Barrett,
There from the Beginning:
Corporate Secretary 1978 – Present,
Vice President Administration 1986 – 1990
Executive Vice President Customers 1990 – 2001,
First Woman President 2001 – Present
Member Board of Directors,
Member Executive Planning Committee,
And
Our Heroine of the Heart Forever

Over the years many skeptics have doubted that Southwest Airlines could keep such a warm, big-hearted, personal culture alive while the Company blossomed like a Texas bluebonnet in springtime, doubling in size again and again. But Colleen and Herb teamed with everyone to make every challenge an opportunity for a new creative solution. Not long after the Culture Committee began, the members expanded this idea to each location and started 63 local Culture Committees built on the same concepts. So now there is a vibrant network teaming to keep work fun, identify and solve emerging problems, ask for help, offer support, and keep alive that unmatched spirit that sets Southwest Airlines apart.

Servant leadership is about developing and encouraging others to lead. Colleen Barrett has an enormous task to keep a Company of 32,000 Employees motivated and 96.4 million Customers happy. How does she do it? She grows, inspires, and supports others to become the Warrior Spirit, lead with a Servant's Heart, and do all of this with a Fun-LUVing Attitude. That's servant leadership in action. That's the Spirit of Southwest!

TAKE AWAYS
TO PONDER

1. Who might you pull together in your organization to begin to define, model, and nurture the spirit of servant leadership?

2. Where and how can you practice "seeing things whole" by gathering People from all sides of a concern to listen respectfully to each other and generate win/win solutions?

3. How can you bring a spirit of fun and appreciation to your work and to those you work with?

4. How can you create fun ways to teach the complexities of your business so that every Employee can learn to think and act like an owner?

5. Southwest created the Triple Crown Challenge, to make it a spirited game to become first in three important metrics in their industry: most on-time flights, least lost baggage, and fewest Customer complaints. How could you create a similar challenge to focus your Employees on critical business goals in a way that highlights fun and teamwork?

6. Southwest looks for ways to make holidays special for their Employees and Customers. Who could help you brainstorm ideas for transforming holidays into creative Employee- or Customer-appreciation events?

A Fractal Forms:
The Servant Leadership
Learning Community

Great ideas, it has been said, come into the world as gently as doves.
Perhaps then, if we listen attentively, we shall hear, amid the uproar of
empires and nations, a faint flutter of wings, the gentle stirring of life and
hope. Some will say that this hope lies in a nation; others, in a [person].
I believe rather that it is awakened, revived, nourished by millions of
solitary individuals whose deeds and works every day negate frontiers
and the crudest implications of history. As a result, there shines forth
fleetingly the ever threatened truth that each and every person, on the
foundation of [one's] own sufferings and joys, builds for all.

Albert Camus in *Resistance, Rebellion and Death*

These stories from the Servant Leadership Learning Community exemplify what Camus was talking about. They illustrate a philosophy of life, a way of living and working for the benefit of others that has been espoused from ancient times. Seventh century B.C. philosopher Lao Tzu counseled:

> *Go to the people – learn from them – live with them;*
> *Start with what they know; build with what they have. . . .*
> *But of the best leaders, when the job is done, when the task is*
>   *accomplished,*
> *The people will all say, "We have done this ourselves."*

In the 20th century, Robert K. Greenleaf chose the term *servant leadership* to give expression to a paradox he found to be true of the best leaders: they are servants first. To Greenleaf, leading was not about a personal quest for power, prestige, or material rewards. It was about growing people and serving the best interests of all.

"The best test, and difficult to administer, is: do those served grow as persons; do they while being served, become healthier, wiser, freer, more autonomous, more likely themselves to become servants? And, what is the effect on the least privileged in society; will each benefit, or at least, not be further deprived?"

Robert K. Greenleaf

Here is a lifetime challenge for anyone who seeks to follow in the footsteps of great leaders. Beginning with ourselves, we can take ownership of our time on earth to benefit the people around us and leave the world a better place because of our presence. We can seek that place where "our deepest joy meets the world's deepest need," to borrow from the writer Frederick Buechner.

The American fixation with heroes who we hope will lead us out of trouble into "life, liberty and the pursuit of happiness" persists. But servant-leaders are typically ordinary people who lift others to new levels of possibility, the outcome of which goes far beyond what one person might accomplish alone or as a boss. They build for all, with often-unnoticed, everyday attitudes and actions. Some recognized traits of servant-leaders include

- Developing self-awareness and humility
- Growing deep mutual trust
- Listening to others first to understand
- Using power ethically, primarily through persuasion
- Seeking consensus when possible
- Utilizing the art of withdrawal to reorient and refresh
- Accepting others, empathizing
- Conceptualizing, seeing the whole and representation of the whole in the parts
- Sharing big-picture information and business strategy broadly
- Being coachable and welcoming feedback.

- Asking what is the right thing to do for all stakeholders, especially those unable to represent their rights and needs
- Defining profit beyond the financial to also include meaningful work, environmental responsibility, and quality of life for all stakeholders.
- Nurturing community

A few years ago, scandalous behavior by some of our top leaders in both public and private sectors highlighted the fact that unethical leadership is not leadership at all.

> "There's a movement in America that insists arrogance, greed, and selfishness don't have to be the hallmarks of business. It's a model of management that's catching on with corporations today called, 'servant leadership.'"
>
> Stone Phillips, News Anchor, "Dateline"

Workers today are searching for leaders who will enable them to grow, personally and professionally. At the same time, many leaders are acknowledging that they lead best by serving others. As Herb Kelleher, Chairman of Southwest Airlines has said, "I have always believed that the best leader is the best server. And if you're a servant, by definition, you're not controlling."

Three Streams Converge: Origins of the SLLC

By the end of the 20th century, the stream of servant leadership consciousness and practice was surging across the globe. Contemporary with the publication of *The Fifth Discipline,* by Peter Senge and his colleagues at M.I.T, another stream within management/organizational theory gained momentum. The AMCA team stepped into this "learning organization" stream early on and began practicing the five disciplines. AMCA also joined the Society of Organizational Learning (SoL) as a way to stay current in our capacity building and to share from our Client work.

Then, in January 1999, a third stream burst forth as *Fortune* magazine published its first survey of "100 Best Companies to Work for in America." The "great places to work" criteria honored two of our long-term Clients (Southwest Airlines, #2, and TDIndustries, #4).

Almost immediately we were inundated with calls from organizations large and small, eager to learn more about servant leadership. Many were small businesses or community organizations whose budgets couldn't support the kinds of comprehensive development curriculums we had co-designed with TD and SWA.

The convergence of these three streams within AMCA opened an opportunity to share what we had learned as practitioners of servant leadership, in addition to the learning organization disciplines, with those who wanted to create great places to work. We made a team decision to co-create a circle of leaders as learning partners and give our time, resources, and facilitation as a gift to the community.

SLLC Members in Dialogue

From our work with SoL, we also learned about "fractals" (learning communities, each of which replicates the pattern of the larger organization) and wondered if this circle of leaders could be an experimental fractal focused on servant leadership woven seamlessly with the five disciplines of a learning organization.

What is now called the Servant Leadership Learning Community officially began in 2000 with seven member organizations and has since grown to 11. Governance has been by consensus, with all members contributing topics and resources for the quarterly meetings. AMCA Partner Gary Looper serves as our SLLC Guide, and AMCA maintains a facilitator role, sharing 30 years of experience creating interactive learning environments to grow and deepen servant leadership.

TD and SWA have also shared a wealth of insights from their 35 and 25 years (respectively), of growing leaderful cultures. As a part of this collaboration, TD generously opened their own servant leadership classes as a lab school (on a space available basis) to members of SLLC.

In SLLC's fifth year, we began inviting host member to share some of their lessons learned, as they applied what we were experiencing together inside their organizations. The results, some of which are included in the previous chapters, have been stunning and inspiring. These are remarkable stories of ordinary people creating extraordinary results as servant leaders.

Today, we continue to "slow down to go faster," to dialogue about current challenges and deepen our ability to serve others as a learning community. We continue to share our discoveries through the global network of SoL and the international Greenleaf Centers for Servant-Leadership.

One of our assumptions over the years has been that we can accomplish far more together than we ever could working separately. If you long to share this journey of servant leadership with others throughout the year, there is no reason why you couldn't start your own local learning community. If you are willing to begin with yourself and then reach out to diverse others, you, too, can co-create a network of support and inquiry. Margaret Mead so wisely observed that it only takes a "small group of dedicated individuals to change the world." If not now, when? If not us, who?

SLLC Members in Dialogue

TAKE AWAYS
TO PONDER

1. It begins with a vision to recruit a community of learning partners. Who in your area might have skills and experiences in consulting in servant leadership and *The Fifth Discipline* (or similar skills in leadership development based on trust and improving communication)?

2. Is there a college, university, or community college where a professor who shares your interest in servant leadership might serve as a host facilitator or sponsor?

3. Look for potential partners with resources to contribute. One secret is to leverage strength through difference.

4. How can you discover those who might share your interest in servant leadership? Local chapters of human resource professionals, women in business, and women and minority-owned businesses could be a place to begin.

SLLC Vision

We aspire to practice and improve our collective skills as a learning community centered on servant leadership. We desire to increase our ability to co-create a future based on relationships of trust and respect as well as a triple bottom line that includes both tangible and intangible benefits for our Employees, Customers, Community, and World.

SLLC Purpose

- To connect with organizational leaders in the Dallas community who share a long-term commitment to developing leaderful cultures (by meeting as a whole group quarterly)

- To deepen our collective servant leadership and learning (by sharing resources such as videos, books, articles, websites, introducing advanced skills, and dialoguing on current challenges and successes)

- To collect stories of servant leadership in the workplace

- To identify the developmental stages of servant leadership that could guide our leadership strategies

- To encourage the hearts of leaders to continue the journey

- To actively practice the five disciplines of a learning community

- To share what we learn through SoL with a broader international community

- To explore what it would mean to become accountable to a triple bottom line of People, Profit, and Planet (sustainability)

SLLC Strategic Questions for Dialogue

These were questions that launched our research as we formed the SLLC. In the years since, we have found good evidence that the answers are positive.

1. Can we leverage stages of development in the long-term growth of a leaderful culture so that those organizations new to this transformation can move more effectively on this journey? (Can a 30-year transformation such as TDIndustries' journey to become a leaderful culture happen more quickly in other organizations?)

2. Are there practices, tools, and lessons learned that we can share for mutual gain?

3. Can we improve the impact of personal and team awareness and transformation by reflecting together to discern patterns and insights we might not pick up separately?

4. Can we share resources and influences to deepen and strengthen the impact across organizations?

Current SLLC Organizational Members

Ann McGee-Cooper and Associates, Inc.

Balfour Beatty
> *(formerly Centex Construction Company)*

Bill Priest Institute for Economic Development

Carrollton Police Department

Celebration Restaurant & Catering

Parkland Health & Hospital System

PCI the data company

Southwest Airlines

TDIndustries

Tempo Mechanical Services

US Cellular

Afterword

By Don M. Frick

Don M. Frick is author of *Robert K. Greenleaf: A Life of Servant Leadership*, the authorized biography of the businessman who first wrote about the idea of the servant as leader.

Reading these remarkable stories reminds me of a Greenleaf quote: "Awareness is a disturber," and several lines from the poem "Stages," by Hermann Hesse:

> Serenely let us move to distant places
> And let no sentiments of home detain us.
> The Cosmic Spirit seeks not to restrain us
> But lifts us stage by stage to wider spaces.
> If we accept a home of our own making,
> Familiar habit makes for indolence.

Heightened awareness of reality, in all its shining and dark dimensions, disturbs us enough to want change. Steve Saunders learned that change can be dramatic *and* that accepting it and working out the details can be slow and crisply painful. While change takes its time to seep into our hearts and policies, leaders and followers work in a swamp that is stripped of familiar road signs; they fight the quicksand suction that makes it difficult to put one foot in front of another, swat the pesky mosquitoes of legal and personal challenges, and keep an eye out for deadly snakes that would end the journey with a fateful bite. But swamps are also some of the most fertile places on earth, full of buzzing, dripping, humming life.

Hermann Hesse, whose character Leo in *Journey to the East* inspired Greenleaf to coin the phrase servant-leader, puts it all in a spiritual perspective: "The Cosmic Spirit seeks not to restrain us/But lifts us stage by stage to wider spaces." The servant-leader's journey parallels the shaman's journey: death, dismemberment, journey to the other side of the sun, and rebirth. The servant-leader keeps dying to the old self. She dismembers familiar habits that make for indolence, like impatience, inattentive listening, and coercive use of power. She goes away to the other side of the sun, where silence and intuition can work their wisdom, and then comes back revivified. There are two alternatives to this kind of positive, courageous life of change – bitterness and depression, or a perfect state of balance called death.

As we see in these stories, people who act as servant-leaders are occasionally thought to be nutty. Servant leadership is a scandal that challenges the common-sense notions of power and leadership. Carrollton Police Chief David James and Mac Tristan risked tampering with the traditional command/control model of police work and moved from a reactive to a proactive stance, resulting in a 94 percent reduction of vehicle thefts. Ed Lowe and John Stout gave control to the bilingual folks who did the tough galley work, thereby saving an important Customer and learning that being a servant-leader means "respecting Employees to help find the answers."

And Jack Lowe, Sr.'s final thoughts about the mission of the company he founded did not even mention profits: "To serve God. To serve our fellow [beings]. To build a group of people who work together in friendship and love." Scandalous. And marvelous.

Every organization needs to evolve its own ways of embracing servant leadership. Dr. Ron Anderson, M.D., and Dr. Jacqualene Stephens, Ph.D., perhaps remembering that "culture eats strategy for lunch," have used servant leadership to persistently change the culture of Parkland Hospital to a tipping point where a critical mass of servant-leaders cascades benefits to Employees and Patients.

I have been privileged to know the authors of this book for some years and honored to meet a number of the people they have profiled. I can tell you this: They are all joyful, not in the shallow way that a cute phrase about the essence of leadership makes one joyful, but in the bone-deep way that a person on the servant-leader journey is joy-filled with humility that keeps them from being impressed by their own titles, with an engaging spirit that uplifts everyone in the room, and with love that is deep enough to give outrageously *and* expect accountability from self and others. In the pre-9/11 days I flew Southwest Airlines one Easter Sunday. Just as the plane was being pushed out of the gate an Employee hopped out of an overhead baggage compartment dressed in a bunny suit! It would not have surprised me if Colleen Barrett herself had hopped down the aisle behind her. That kind of joy.

Read these stories again for the lessons, and yet again to be inspired – again.

Index

Acknowledgments

We want to thank Harriet Lowe for introducing Ann to her husband Jack Lowe, Sr., and planting the seeds that led to this journey. Jack Lowe, Sr., was a great inspiration to us all as is his son, Jack Lowe, Jr., who never wavered in his belief and support for servant leadership and our work, especially when there were big financial challenges. We also thank TDIndustries CEO, Harold MacDowell, who continues to champion servant leadership along with three decades of TD Partners, including Jessie McCain, Bob Ferguson, and Ben Houston.

Steve Saunders was Ann's first teaching partner at TD. Initially he helped in many ways and has been a founding member of SLLC. We thank all the members of SLLC and especially those who have hosted our sessions and shared their internal stories, six of which are featured in this book.

Dr. Ron Anderson, Jacqualene Stephens, and Linda Wilkerson continue to bring great courage and vision to our work together at Parkland Health & Hospital System. The story we share from Parkland is a tribute to these three remarkable servant-leaders and all those who model the Parkland Way.

We honor and thank Police Chief David James and Assistant Police Chief Mac Tristan and all the line officers who volunteer in the Community Problem-Oriented Policing (CPOP) Team.

Ed Lowe and his team of inspiring Partners at Celebration Restaurant continue to earn a reputation as a leaderful company, a great place to work, and a wonderful venue to enjoy a delicious meal.

And at Southwest Airlines, we thank Sunny Abercrombie, Director of the Culture Committee, and key leaders, including Joyce Rogge, Tonda Montague, Donna Conover, Jeff Lamb, Cheryl Hughey, Dave Ridley, Cynthia Young, Ellen Torbert, Jim Wimberly, and Jim Sokol for their insights from many years working directly with Colleen Barrett, now President of SWA. We also thank Ginger Hardage and Brian Lusk for helping to ensure the accuracy of our Southwest Airlines chapter.

We are indebted to our three mentors from Singapore, Hee Piang Chin, Low Guat Tin, and Sally Chew-Ong Gek Tee, who supported the vision for this book at the Greenleaf Conference in June, 2006, after we reported on the Servant Leadership Learning Community. "Ann, you and your AMCA, Inc., Partners must tell these stories and have your book ready for the 2007 Conference." We are grateful for their encouragement and inspiring role model. These courageous servant-leaders are growing the commitment and passion to serve others around the world.

We are grateful to Don Frick, Herb Zureich, and Deborah Vogel Welch, who served as readers and provided thoughtful feedback. We also thank editor, Deborah Costenbader, who brought clarity to the writing, Suzanne Pustejovsky-Perry for creative cover design, and Timm Chamberlain for elegant book design and layout.

And finally, we thank Larry Cooper for 25 years of support and our AMCA Partners, Carol Haddock, Justin Davis, and Lolita Trammell for your sense of humor and daring to believe in and fully support this bold dream.

The Authors

Ann McGee-Cooper, Ed.D., is founding Partner of Ann McGee-Cooper & Associates, a team of futurists and consultants. She is an international leader in researching and applying servant leadership in the workplace, having served on the Culture Committee of Southwest Airlines for 16 years and with TDIndustries for 30 years. She has counseled national business leaders, governmental officials and college presidents on servant leadership, culture transformation, high-performance teaming, life/work balance, time management, and creative problem solving and is author of *You Don't Have To Go Home From Work Exhausted, Time Management For Unmanageable People* and *The Essentials of Servant-Leadership: Principles in Practice.*

Gary Looper, Th.M., serves as Project Leader of the pacesetting Servant Leadership Learning Community, a consortium of 11 organizations that meet together during the year to develop unique, leaderful cultures and the learning organization disciplines. He also serves as Project Manager and Director of Publications for AMCA. He is co-author of the IMS monograph, *The Essentials of Servant Leadership: Principles in Practice* (Pegasus Communications).

Duane Trammell, M.Ed., founding Partner and Executive Vice President of AMCA, has been working with Ann for 25 years. He manages the operations and finances of the company. With a Master's degree in Gifted Education and Supervision, Duane has taken a special interest in writing, researching, and developing materials in servant leadership. He has co-authored *Time Management for Unmanageable People*, and *You Don't Have To Go Home from Work Exhausted!* Trammell led our team in the development of 14 modules designed with an interactive approach to teaching servant leadership. As an award-winning educator, business trainer and seminar facilitator, Duane's specialty is implementing creative ideas and translating theory into practical business applications.

More About Ann McGee-Cooper and Associates, Inc.

AMCA, Inc. is a team of organizational consultants specializing in servant leadership and offering client services in leadership development, culture transformation, team alignments, executive coaching, and keynote/seminar presentations.

Two of AMCA's longest clients/partners, TDIndustries and Southwest Airlines, have been in the top five of Fortune's "100 Best Companies to Work for in America" list.

To find out how your organization can benefit from AMCA's experience, call 214-357-8550 or visit our website, www.amca.com.

More Servant Leadership Products from AMCA, Inc.

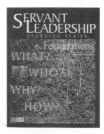  

These modules are a collection of 30 years of research growing servant leadership in business, education, religious, health care, and government organizations. Each module (approximately 45 to 90 minutes in length) is designed to be taught alone or in sequence with other modules. A facilitator's guide provides directions for an interactive learning approach to engage participants as they connect servant leadership to their life and work.

Each notebook includes four learning modules with facilitator instructions.

Price: $99.00 each.

CALL AMCA, Inc. 214-357-8550